Sunflower Facing the Sun

Winner of the Edwin Ford Piper Poetry Award

Publication of this book was made possible with the

generous assistance of Janet Piper

POEMS BY GREG PAPE

Sunflower
Facing the Sun

University of Iowa Press Ψ Iowa City

University of Iowa Press, Iowa City 52242

Copyright © 1992 by Greg Pape

Printed in the United States of America

Design by Richard Hendel

Printed on acid-free paper

96 95 94 93 92 P 10 9 8 7 6 5 4 3 2 1

Library of Congress Cataloging-in-Publication Data

Pape, Greg, 1947–

   Sunflower facing the sun: poems/by Greg Pape

      p.   cm.—(Edwin Ford Piper poetry award)

   ISBN 0-87745-382-9

   I. Title. II. Series.

PS3566.A614S8 1992   92-5881

811'.54—dc20   CIP

FOR MARNIE AND COLEMAN AND CLAY

Acknowledgments

My thanks to the editors of the following publications in which these poems first appeared.

Colorado Review:
   "Church," "Cows"
Cutbank:
   "Blessing at the Citadel"
Kinnikinnik:
   "The Gravest of Wishful Thinking"
Mid-American Review:
   "The Big One," "In the Bluemist Motel"
Poetry:
   "Morning of the First Birth"
Wilderness:
   "Whitetails"

Contents

IV. TOWARD YOU

V. RUINS

PART ONE

¡Viva la Huelga!

Desert Motel before Dawn

Up at 4:00 A.M., an hour and a half
or a lifetime of darkness yet to come,
the sun just touching the waves
breaking on the Atlantic shore,
or blocked by clouds reluctant
to let the light down on avenues
already crowded with workers.
Here, others stir in the rooms, brothers,
sisters, fellow workers who, for a moment
as they try to shake off one dream
and slip into another, don't know who
or where they are. California City,
they were told, but who can be sure?
This room is familiar and anonymous,
the No Tell Motel anchored to the desert
with cement, a small idea that hardens,
and stapled into a box to keep out
most of the wind, sun, and hordes
of desert tortoises that come out
after the rains. This room among rooms
stocked with cheap beds remade each noon,
prepared by a maid from Coahuila
for the marriage of heaven and hell.

Pickups idle in the parking lot, workers
fill the big aluminum coolers
with gallons of water, the cook in the cafe
lays out the lines of bacon
and beats the eggs. A waitress downs
her coffee, lights her second cigarette,

and says here they come again Jesus to no one.
We should probably stop here
and leave them to their breakfast,
the tedious work ahead, the sorry jokes
no one needs to hear.
We could go back to the motel together
where a couple not unlike ourselves
have been up and down all night,
soldiers in the war for peace and happiness,
laborers at love working away the darkness
between them, whipping up the winds
that keep the body turning, making the sun
shine and the rains rain,
freeing the hordes and the angels
who may or may not come.

Coldburn Vertigo

There was a wind of faces
passing in the street,
a chill rippling of bodies in the glass,
eyes that closed or burned
when he looked into them.
The women were angry or stoned,
so were the men.
There were no children.
The old ones leaned into the wind
or hung their heads over the pavement
as though looking for a single blade
of grass or tuft of weed
that might return them to the home
their bodies had been.

A woman dropped her purse
in a crosswalk. He bent
to pick it up. She screamed
in his face. His heart shrank,
his body went gray and small,
his eyes, round and bald
in the wind. He darted
among the trod and footfall
gurgling and cooing over cracks
and stained slabs.

Then he found a door
under spitting blue neon,
the Lion's Den, the Lamb's Pen,
he wasn't sure. He opened the door,

took twelve or fourteen steps,
and settled himself on a stool
in the smokey blue gloom.
In the mirror across the bar,
a small man in a helmet of feathers
closed his burning eyes.

Vertigo reeked from some ashtray
in his brain. He drifted up
and rippled like a ribbon of smoke
on that warm air that was breath
turned to words turned to surf,
the hiss and roar, the undertone
in all the rooms wearing at the thin,
sheer membrane of the eardrum,
the swirl and rush in the blood
that is the wind in the streets,
waves working at every shore.

Who was he but this man adrift,
this man turned into a pigeon
drawn by desire and contagion
to streets and gutters and smokey rooms,
the fascinating city, away from the boy
whose mother loved him, the boy
who held the heads of the electric cat,
the tender dog against his chest
because they consented, because they seemed
to understand the simple rhythm

of his heart, the choice he had made
with his hands.

When he opened his eyes,
things went from bad to worse
to a kind of cold burning
in which he found himself
hovering in the dark
near the ceiling just above
the blue shower pouring from the spotlight
onto the naked, dancing woman.
She was not really a woman
but a holograph of a woman
jerking to a drumbeat that erased her
and left this cold, still-lovely body
burning in her place.

She was less than a woman,
he was less than a man.
In something less than this life,
drifting down through the music
in his garment of feathers,
he alighted among the glitter
in her hair, and his eyes
were two more points of blue light
burning, blue gas flames
in some far room.

And just when he thought it was over,
just when the cymbals shimmered
like water on fire
and the small room of his mind dimmed,
he felt her hand around him,
his bird-heart beating with the drum
in the room gone red,
and she held him to her breast
and danced as though she were real,
as though even this moment mattered.

¡Viva la Huelga!

There was resentment and pride
in the way they waved the red flag
so that the blocky black wings
of the symbol that stood for the eagle
flapped and pushed at the angry red air,
trying to fly.

I thought I was just going to work,
finally, after all those mornings
standing in line to earn again
my weekly check, twenty-nine dollars,
after all those forms and phone calls
and interviews in which the questions
and the answers feel like lies
even when they are true, and the one
who asks and the one who answers
are both liars by omission.
That year it seemed the whole San Joaquin,
my valley, my state, my country,
my own eyes were all liars by omission.
The woman who loved me was exempt,
and each morning when I rose to
and from her body, my own body
was a gift she had given me.

That year I read some great books,
burned my draft card, and lamented
all the deaths that weren't mine
and the one that was. That year
I got a job working for an entrepreneur

farmer, inventor of a mechanical peach harvester.
For two weeks we trained for the day
of its demonstration. Each morning when the sun
rose over the Sierras, we tucked our pants
into our boots, tied bandanas over our faces,
pulled the gloves over our cuffs, grabbed hold
of the clamp handles on the hydraulic arms,
and swung our shakers down the rows
like machine gunners attacking the trees.
Clouds of fuzz rose as peaches fell in the heat,
and sweat meant to cool the body
turned to mold. By noon each day,
we had shaken the peaches from a dozen rows
of trees and all the thoughts out of our minds.

When the big day arrived
and we drove slowly up the dirt road
trailering the harvester behind the truck
between the rows of solemn peach trees
and angry people waving the red flag
with the black eagle, shouting ¡Viva la Huelga!
I stared at them like the daydreamer I was,
a young man dreaming his lover next to him
in a summer orchard who leans over
and looks into his eyes, but instead
of parting her lips for the deep kiss
that leads to heaven, she slaps him hard
in the face to awaken him to shame.

Storm Surf

Rumor had it there had been
a hell of a storm or a tsunami
somewhere out in the Pacific,
one of those big, restless spirits
that visit the earth and carry off
whole populations and make a sudden mess
of everything in their path.
I stood on the beach with a borrowed board,
watching the great waves that dwarfed the pier
rise like glassy cliffs out of the fog.
I counted four or five surfers out there,
and now and then I saw one paddling hard
up a wave-face or streaking across a wall
in a crouch and disappearing in a tunnel
turning back into a wall. He was out there
somewhere, my mentor, the one I wanted
to be. We were to meet just offshore
of the continent, outside the farthest breaker,
there on the deep and restless, the saltwater
of origins and fates where we would ride
the elemental power of the turning earth,
our eyes, ears, mouths, hearts, and arms
open to fathom the purpose of the air
this very morning at eight. I waited,
shivering in my baggies, for a lull in the waves.

I took ten deep breaths, then ten more,
slow as resolve, and hit the water running
and bellied the board through the shore-break

and paddled out over the hiss and blather
of the soup that sounded like a chorus of the drowned.
I worked through the inside break, pumping
and paddling over crests, doing Hawaiian rolls,
washing back shoreward, half-flipping up
for air, laying a tired cheek on the grains
of sand caught in the paraffin until
what was grace was revised, and so much
effort made up of slight mistakes
in the face of a greater force turned
to doubt in the lines of sight glinting
from the brain, in the strings that pulled
the muscles that fumbled the strokes.
Grace changed too much may still
resemble grace, but hints of damage
in the way it moves.

It's hard to tell now, but it must have taken
an hour to get out past the pier
where the big waves rose stone-faced
out of the fog, not quite ready to break.
I straddled the board, rising up faces
and falling in troughs and calling
to the others, who must have had their fill
of doubt and secret glory and somehow
made it in while I, foolish, made it out.
The waves kept coming and breaking
before me until, even in the fog,

I could see clearly now the one I wanted to be,
beached and breathing, savoring the simple,
holding the broken halves of moments
carried out of the sea in strong
but humble arms.

Some Names

Nooncaster, Colombini, Abrahms, Perez,
Patigian, Doohan, Eliot, Masterpolo,
Roderick, some names come back tonight.
Nooncaster was a butcher
who drove a red Corvette with a fiberglass
body that shattered like a toy. He always
carried cash, supplied every barbecue
with fresh red meat, and charmed the air
with his quick delivery, bright eyes,
and the odd music—part nasal, part gravel—
of his voice. Colombini had biceps
like baseballs. Abrahms was an unlit
neon sign who could turn it on
when he wanted to and sing like Sam Cooke
or Otis Redding long before they were ghosts,
but spent most of his time in a dark dream
of some childhood road listening. Perez
was cool, no better word for the way
he moved through the hot valley nights
in spit-shined french toes or a lowered
Chevy black as his eyes, his hair slicked back
as if to say the wind, sun, moon, and stars
all stop when I stop. Patigian
was part lion, part wren, but looked
like a bear. Doohan lit the barbecue
with gas splashed from a baby moon hubcap,
and just as we imagined it would happen,
his arm went up in flames. Eliot
drove his loaded Ford on country roads
and raced the trains to crossings

and almost always won. Masterpolo
made a mess of things in the Y Knot Roadhouse
because he wouldn't let it ride, he tore
the antlered heads from the dumb walls.
Old friends, acquaintances, role models
in the badass arts of adolescence.
And Roderick, we called him Red, had
a fine, nervous laugh and hands
quick enough to confuse even his own freckles.
Roderick, one of those names on the wall
in Washington you can find in your own face.

In the Bluemist Motel

I hear voices in the next room
that stop and the closing of a door
in the Bluemist Motel in Florence, Arizona,
across the road from the state penitentiary,
where I am about to close the venetian blinds
to mute the light that shines all night
from the guard towers and the sign.
In this room, I imagine, two brothers
plotted the escape of their father
who had murdered a man in a rage
but had always loved his boys.
They made it almost to Gallup
before their stolen van was stopped
at a roadblock, just north of the Río Puerco
on Defiance Plateau, and the shooting began.
One of the boys took a bullet in the brain
and died there under the stars and shattered
glass. Now, the other brother and the father
live in separate cells across the road
and listen, as I do, at intervals all night
to the metallic voice of the loudspeaker
giving instructions in numbers and code.
This is years ago as I stand at the window
with the cord in my hand dusted blue
from the neon sign that buzzes over
the parking lot and the locked cars.
I don't know why all this comes back
tonight, insistent, as if I might
have done something to change the course
of these lives. As if I might have stepped in

between the father and the man he was about
to murder and said something strong and final
so that the father turned away in shame
and the sheriff never pulled the trigger
and the boy is still walking around somewhere
with a perfectly good brain he's finally
learning how to use, and his brother
has decided to marry again for the second
or third time and, because he's put in
a good day's work and he's tired, the father
is falling asleep in his own bed.

Medicine

When Stan and I lifted our paddles
and let the yellow canoe glide
over the shallow water of the flats
beyond the mangroves of Buck Key,
and the great flock of roseate spoonbills,
whom I know now are the *Ajaia ajaja*
of the family Threskiornithidae,
lifted their heads, swayed and dipped
in unison, extended their wings, flapped,
stroked, and rose like a blushing cloud
into the pink clouds of sunset over the Gulf,
all the infirmities of nine years of childhood
were healed by the medicine of that moment.
Or so it seemed.

            Later in Los Angeles,
a friend to all dogs, they shaved my head
so that I had to wear a longshoreman's cap
to school and suffer the mild and unmild
abuse of my peers, and twice a week
have my head painted green
with something cold and unpronounceable
and sit for a long time alone
holding the odd encumbrance of my head
still beneath the ultraviolet glow
buzzing from the contraption hung
from the dark ceiling in the closed room
they said was medicine, where I wept
for the tenderness of dogs, the power of birds,
and the unpredictable nature of all things.

PART TWO

In the Birthing Room

Morning of the First Birth

She wakes before dawn,
not quite alone in an upstairs room
of a blue house, and breathes out
the apprehensions and in the hopes
of that house above the braided channels
of the river moving through the valley
between the abruptly rising
Bitterroot range and the rounded,
hilly shapes of the Sapphires.
She feels a dampness beneath her
on the sheets and begins to suppose.

She has come down the stairs
and stands beside the bed
where he lies on his right side
curled in a sleeping bag. Light
from the sun that rose over the Sapphires
an hour ago shines through the east window
and touches his night-tousled hair.
She thinks it's a good sign. No storm
today. No black ice on the roads.
She stands a moment more, looking at him,
feeling a globe lightness turning
planet heavy. Then she wakes him,
and tells him it's time.

He stands until steam rises,
then steps into the rush of water
that wakes his skin. He thinks of a song,
"Many Rivers to Cross," but doesn't sing.

He reaches for the soap and washes
quickly as his mind begins to race
with the things he must do because today
is the day.

She is talking on the phone to someone
at the hospital twenty miles north.
She is saying yes to questions
and someone is saying yes to her.

They walk out together into the day,
this man and this woman with a child
stirring in her body, carrying the weight
and promise of all the days
since the day they first beheld each other
in a parking lot in San Antonio.

They look at each other differently now,
and the question they don't ask
is there before them. The answer is yes.
Yes is the word, made with so little breath,
indrawn or expelled. Yes, smallest of winds
that set a life in motion,
on which a life depends.

In the Birthing Room

You can say anything, but there are things
that can't be told. They've worked out a method
of breathing to help you through, to ease the pain,
but the pain is deeper than breath goes.
I'll never know. Here, for me, things
are as simplified as a traffic light,
the quickly passing yellow of choice
between two commands. Here's my hand.
Nothing can drive me away.
I am like a stud in the wall
that makes this room possible.
You are like a sunflower facing the sun.
For better or worse, here for the duration.
Let the knees buckle, the hernia bulge,
the sweat swim along the lines of the skin.
Let the discs of the spine fuse
with cold fire, let the feet flatten,
and the small vessels in the eyes burst
and redden. Listen to the voice of the will,
egged on by the heart, setting out
on this journey through the mountains,
deserts, and swamps of the body.
I'll hold your hand, and fan and fan
for as many hours as it takes.
This is December tenth and January twenty-eighth.
This is the day within the days
we've been moving toward.

Nurse says don't push, resist the urge
to push. Doctor says push.
I say breathe, breathe.
You open your mouth, release another mottled
sparrow of pain. You can say anything.

Among the Various Errors

I've gone down into the river
to see what it's like to be a fish.
Shadows of wings have passed over me
and I've hidden in fear.
I've seen nymphs swim up from the rocks
toward the light, seen the delicate ones
move in the meniscus, and I've risen
to take them in my mouth.
I've felt the terror of the hook
and the pull of the tight line.
I've broken free and lay stunned
on the bottom, pumping my red gills
to live. I've quivered in the hand
and beheld the eyes of the man I am.
All this among the various errors
and insights of the imagination.
I still know almost nothing
about grief, except that it has value
and can't be thrown away, and
laughter is a kind of water
that riffles over the rocks
and shines.

■

My friend told the story of a lonely man
who found a dead baby in the can
and took it home and washed it carefully,
wrapped it in a clean towel, held it gently,
and wept all day
until the police came and took it away.

■

When my son was born, he spent a long time
in the birth canal. His mother would push
and the top of his head would appear, crowning,
then disappear. It seemed like hours
before he was all the way born into the one
good hand of the doctor on duty, who held
my son's head down a moment, wiped clear
the nostrils so the first breath swelled
his small chest, his eyes opened, and he
looked around the room in true wonder.
I laughed with relief when he released
a tiny stream, a small, golden arc of triumph.

■

The doctor placed him on his mother's belly
and turned away, and in that slippery moment,
he slid off between her legs
and fell through the close air down
into the bottom of a plastic trash bag
placed there over a hamper to catch the placenta.
The doctor fished him quickly out by one
tiny arm. After that the doctor wouldn't
look at me. I might have said something
in anger, but joy still held my tongue.
I cut the cord, shook the doctor's good hand.
I tell the story now, and laugh,
how my firstborn son slipped
from his mother into the trash.

Church

Tarnished fake gold chains and cross,
dirty gold tangles of hair

around a bruised, sun-scabbed face
in which the eyes sputter

but burn like an arc welder under water,
one I-could-cut-your-throat hand

in a pocket, the other whispering
help me please through the dead Los Angeles air,

he comes toward me, father
holding my son in my arms, son

for whose sake I feel a sudden
ferocity pulse through my heart

as he steps quickly toward us through still air
soon to rise from the oil-stained asphalt

of this parking lot warming in morning sun,
this church where I offer the coins

and receive his blessing
and we hold each other

a moment only among the uncommitted
murders in our eyes.

The Gravest of Wishful Thinking

Even before Marnie came through the door
   crying Greg Greg we've got an emergency
and adrenaline knocked me out of that peace
   that comes from leaning over the cheap
yellow paper and kicked me up the stairs
   in a panic of possibilities,
even before I saw the fright in her face,
   the blood, tears, and screams disfiguring
the face of our young son, his free hand
   opening and closing rapidly in pain,
even before I blurted Oh God what
   and the panic in my voice
caused his screams to increase and her voice
   to assume an even tone,
even before I saw the bloodstains on her blouse
   shaped like the unruly, hallucinatory continents
of early explorers, and I took a breath
   and grabbed a towel, the blood
began to slow, the wound to heal.

After the long ride to the hospital, the gusts
and dull vespers of guilt, the relief and the ice,
   I returned to my work and my wishful thinking.
In the blood there is a sun, a moon, and a kind
   of weather that makes everything possible.

For all the right and wrong reasons, for the general
   good, for the democratic way, to combat aggression,
to put the terrorists in their place, to demonstrate
   our will, to protect our interests, to save

our children from the monster we must confront,
    with their bodies and minds, now or later, for God,
for country, for oil, for the terrible fun of it,
    we are poised again for war.

We all know they have called on their God,
    who has whispered encouragement
into the very temple cells of their young bodies.
    We all know the graves
are already prepared and the great hospital ships
    are stocked with morphine and plasma,
scalpels and gauze, bone saws and body bags.
    The letters of notification
are already written. The anchorman,
    the anchorwoman are ready with their fixed gazes
and perfect American. The priests and rabbis
    and mullahs will know what to say
because they have been saying it all along:
    "Verily my love overcometh my anger."
We all know there are oceans of tears
    yet to be cried. But heart and brain,
posed now before us as enemies, may be the most
    powerful allies no matter what land,
language, temple, mosque, body, and the blood
    has secrets it wants to keep.

                    November 2, 1990

Peace

I can see my mother and my wife
sitting in a booth inside the restaurant
eating breakfast as I stand in the parking lot
with my nineteen-month-old son in my arms.
We have stepped out into the morning sun
because he refuses to eat or sit in a high chair
or stop shouting "tractor tractor" at the old man
in a motorized wheelchair trying to read
his paper in peace.

It's peace we want amid the angers
and hungers of this city. For my son,
it's the peace that comes from the release
from confinement and restraint. For myself,
the release, temporarily, from the role
of confiner and restrainer. And those two
women we love, sitting together unlike strangers
at breakfast (we can see only their heads
and shoulders through the window), are remaking
quietly the necessary bonds of family,
brushing off the crumbs of strangeness,
and sipping coffee in a kind of peace
made possible by many choices based on
what we can't see, and what we can.

At the corner of Long Beach Blvd. and Ocean Ave.,
you can see neither ocean nor beach,
but the bow of the *Queen Mary* hulks
in the distance between high rises
from which older men and women have been

evicted so the buildings may be renovated
to further the economic goals of the republic.
My mother, still one of the lucky, has found
a low-rent room on the fourth floor
of Baptist Gardens with a view of a parking lot
where her '67 Pontiac Catalina is parked
and still runs when she needs it.
There is a tree she loves to look down on,
a Mexican market that is usually open,
an intersection with a constant surf of traffic,
and, morning and evening, the warm, soft air
that smells of exhaust and the Pacific.

Travel Day

We have just risen through the clouds
above Spokane.
Inches from my body, on the plane's
aluminum skin, the wind
is stronger than a class five hurricane,
but here it doesn't even rustle
the pages of a magazine.
The clouds are a kind of music now,
rolling below.
Mountains rise to the east
in rhythmic lines.
It would take a whale
to sing the notes that stream north.
We are turning toward the west.
Some of us look out the portholes,
unwilling to give in to the abstract.
Miles above the earth,
we sit in our secret lives, flying
into newspapers and magazines,
or settling lightly on the ground
of sleep.
The young man across the aisle,
crew cut and two weeks beard,
sweatshirt and faded jeans,
black, court-worn hightops, holds
his five-month-old daughter
asleep in his arms.
They are flying to Phoenix
for the first time.

They said goodbye to the tearful
young mother on the blue concourse,
and have given themselves
into a cold winter sky
to be held awhile above the world.

PART THREE

The Call of the Boreal Owl

The Call of the Boreal Owl

The boreal owl is one of the secrets
of the northern forests.
As far as anyone knows,
it is silent for all but two weeks
of the year, and its call, when it calls,
is meant to attract a mate.
In one of the bird books,
the call is described as the tolling
of a soft bell.
I imagined the sound, haunting
and clear, coming from somewhere
in a dark wall of conifers
across moonlit snow, a hollow sound
yet distinct and resonant
out of all proportion to the fist-sized
bell of feathers tolling in the dark
above the snow. It was a sound
like nothing else on earth.
It reminded me of so many things.
I thought of the blue sound of wind
against my coat, the slight whistling sound
of water dripping, and the mating call
of the pigeon strutting under the church bell
above the courtyard and the blindfolded man
standing against the wall
with his hands tied, feeling that sound
like feathers falling on his head
above the doomed pounding of his heart.

Last night above a high,
snow-covered meadow,
I heard the call, a drift of warm notes
in the cold that stopped
when I opened my mouth
to praise the owl's secrecy
and long silence,
the beauty and urgency of its call.

Wading the Bitterroot

He stands ankle deep in the river
watching three or four trout
rising to some unseen insect on the bright surface.
A mink swims toward him
with shining black eyes, an urgent look
as if she has some message,
but stops midstream and turns back.
The riffles sparkle and flash.
The air is still,
then suddenly filled with the wingbeats
of fifty or more mergansers
flying upstream low over the water.
They rise as one
over some invisible hump in the air,
some slight fear,
then angle down close to the surface again.
They turn as the river turns.
He follows the last one around a bend of willows.
The river keeps coming
with its glitter and shine, nymphs struggling
out of their skins, coming up
through the water toward the strong light,
wings unfolding.
Rainbows and cutthroats flash beneath the surface,
feeding on the small bodies.
The tricos are coming off now, rising and falling,
hovering over the water
and along the willows in a growing cloud,
more and more rising in sunlight.
It's like looking into an atom, he thinks, or seeing

a soul take shape.
This is it, he thinks, now, and a big
orange-bellied sucker
swims slowly up unafraid into the shallows
at his feet, looking for a place
to die. His bright green fly line gone slack
along the edge of the current,
he feels his ignorance and his knowledge
like the clear cold
of the water he stands in.
He bows once to the living river,
then wades in deeper.

Whitetails

The husks of yellow berries move
like soundless bells
as their bodies brush against them.
Their scents cling to them like loose
clothing as they cross the road
and slip in among the bare limbs
and dry grass. The snow, old snow,
crunches and creaks beneath them,
and the dense air, cold and still,
holds the sound of their steps
and their breathing. They move
in a line through the trees above
the stream, shadowing the stream's course.
A breath or sigh, some human sound stops
in the air. White tails go up
in warning. The buck glides up
through the trees a few yards
and stops. Three does. Four.
The buck fixes his eyes on a point
above the snow, ears and tail erect,
body poised. I stand still,
returning his stare. He moves
his long, muscled neck with a quick,
birdlike motion once, twice
to fasten his eyes more securely
upon me. And for a moment,
we define each other's world,
joined at eye level and heartbeats
above the snow.

Earth Day 1990

I think I will leave it alone,
leave the planting of trees to someone else.
I won't drive the pickaxe

or work the shovel into the rocky soil.
I won't cut or prune a thing.
For this one day, my observance

will be to leave things alone,
to listen to the falling of the sticky bud scales
of the balsam poplar,

the recitation of the meadowlark,
the windy prayer of the grass.
And when the sun drops

behind the mountains,
I will close my eyes to hold the light
and feel the turning.

Two Hmong Tapestries

A monkey hangs on the limb of a tree
in bloom. Deer bow their heads
to the grass, and other animals stand
poised on a field of blue, some in pairs,
some alone. A bright-eyed tiger gazes
toward the border, the only hint of menace
in this garden with a still pool serene
at the center where a white stork stands
on one leg and looks out at the other world.

In this world my son is new to, it's June
in Montana. A day of wind, sun, and rain
in the Bitterroot. This morning I took him
for his first close look at the river.
Runoff, high water. We drove a dirt road
and parked at the trailhead next to a pasture.
We stood still, Coleman in his pack on my back,
and stared at a herd of Black Angus. Cows
and calves stared back. When a bull bellowed,
I felt my son's small body startle.

On the trail to the river through what was,
not long ago, ceremonial grounds of the Salish,
we came upon a doe browsing the creek bank.
We stopped. She raised her head and moved
her long neck from side to side as though
to separate us from the background, to weigh us
with her eyes. Cottonwood leaves rattled
in the breeze, water moved with a sound
of muted voices.

                                        One step
and the moment was broken. We watched her
bound away, tail waving like a white flag.
On the bank of the Bitterroot, Coleman looked
upriver, then down, then up again, moving
his eyes, like the deer, on the moving body
of water.

I think of the Hmong crossing the Mekong
with their children on their backs. An image
stitched into a tapestry, soldiers with machine
guns and planes driving them from their homes,
destroying their gardens. Some of them died,
some of them lost their minds, some of them
carried the garden with the still pool inside them.

The Jackrabbit's Ears

Why do jackrabbits have such big ears?
I always thought it was because
they liked to sit in the shade
of a creosote bush or a juniper
all day and listen to God
or whatever devil might be hungry
and headed their way.
That's what I do when I sit
at the desk waiting for the spirit
to move me, looking for words
to say whatever it is that needs
to be said. I envy the jackrabbit
his patience and his instinct.
I admire his big ears, ears
the light passes through, ears
that radiate the heat of his body
and cool him without loss
of water, ears he holds erect
at an angle of seventeen degrees
from the north horizon, pointed
precisely at the coolest area of sky,
listening for the exact sound
of the present, and for the life ahead.

La Paz

One by one the divers follow the bubbles
of their breath back to the surface.
They take off their fins, climb aboard the boat,
remove weight belts, tanks, tight rubber suits,
all those awkward adaptations to the sea.

For awhile they talk with much enthusiasm
about what they have seen below. "It's another world
down there," one of them says. A woman
shakes the water from her hair, a man
gestures with his hands, describing the size

and movement of fish and eels. They wrap
themselves in towels and sit down in pairs
to talk, or alone to look out across the water
at the setting sun as the boat rumbles off
toward the port of La Paz over the smooth,

windless sea turning pink as the clouds.
One woman hooks her arms over the starboard
rail, stretches her long legs, relaxes her back,
and gives in to sweet fatigue as the vibrations
from the diesel engine move through her body

as she moves over the sea. She sighs, smiles,
then sticks out her tongue at the camera aimed at her.
On the other side, in another time, I'm following
what the camera recorded, watching her as she turns
her face and looks out over the water

and slips away. The scene tilts and jerks
over the churning water and vanishing V
of the boat wake, then steadies on gulls and jagged rocks
of a shore across miles of water. A man
appears, excited, gesturing to the camera, "Look, look!"

pointing at something, a disturbance in the water.
Dolphins, hundreds of dolphins, a huge herd
breaking the surface, leaping. And whoever holds
the camera is as fascinated as the man is,
as I am, awake late in this snowbound house

where the others are sleeping, gone into themselves
like divers into a world below, and the boat
heads for port surrounded by dolphins smiling
the inscrutable smile of their species, lifting
on their backs the light of a lost day.

And thinking all days will be lost days,
I would hold these two moments
and follow into the currents of sleep
the woman's turning toward the water,
the dolphins leaping at sunset.

PART FOUR

Toward You

Cows

Build a world of cows
and see where it gets you.
My cows, really my neighbor's cows,
move through the day like worlds
unto themselves. Between the fences
they revolve, between night and day
they stand. They stand for the ground
they stand on, they stand for the grass,
green or burned, alive or the sturdy husks
of lives. They stand for the air, the sky,
the weather that shows no mercy.
Over the fields, down the hill to the gully,
up the hill to the hill, they drift like clouds.
They lie down in the sun, suggesting,
at a distance, the first rocks
that came to rest. These cows
stand for the world we build,
and though we see daily the terror
of where we're going, we say more more
like the cows who are, like us,
between the seeds and the flames, a truce.

The Oyster Gatherers

Pines and firs and a blanket of mist
on the water. A gull sets its wings
and drops into the mist and disappears.
I slip out of the sleeping bag

and walk down into the mist
toward the place where the water
must be. The mist is chest deep
and so thick I can't see my feet.

I'm alone in the morning. It's Thursday,
I think, Holy Thursday. I'm free,
with a month of travel before me,
maybe a lifetime of mornings

like this one, for all I know.
I go on walking, my head in the clear,
fragrant air, my body in a cloud
of mist, my feet on the firm mud

of a tidal flat. I stop. Breathe.
Smell the water and the living mud.
Suddenly I hear voices, but look around
and see no one. A head pops up

out of the mist, goes down again,
then another and another. Still half
asleep, my body in the mist, my head
in the light, I step toward them
to learn their secret.

Toward You

I remember a morning of intense heat
in Indio, one hundred and nine degrees
at nine in the morning, and I needed
coffee to keep driving into that wall
of flames that was the desert I love that day.
By noon it was a hundred and nineteen,
and the pickup tore through veil after veil
of rippling air, the road an aluminum ribbon
receding into the distance, the asphalt future
turning to water as I drove through the desert
toward you.

I remember La Veta Pass, stopping
at a roadside spring to fill a jug
and water the dog, and looking
through the clear air of early summer
at the Spanish Peaks, drinking the cold water
that flowed from the side of the mountain,
seeing in the two peaks, for a moment,
an image of marriage, two mountains,
two people, distinct, yet rising together
out of the same rock and ground,
and staying on side by side through the seasons.
And in the next moment, thinking how silly
that vision, how unlike mountains we are,
how that unlikeness makes us love mountains
with an easy constancy.

For E.

I close my eyes and see you.
What clear, dark eyes!
What a smile you have on your face!

The blindfolded woman holding the scale
tipped to one side
by the weight of a sparrow
is only an image in a dream.
Whereas justice
is the indiscriminate hammer of God.

Forgive me, but it hurts.
It hurts to look at the faces
of children whose father
won't be coming home again,
except as a quiet voice
among the orange trees
or the rhythmic *cumbia*
of the crickets at dusk.

The Sign

Fluorescent orange sprayed on a fence post
means no trespassing. We all know that.
You could say it's the product of a culture,
not a single man. But the rancher
down the wet end of Dry Gulch doesn't
trust us to acknowledge the sanctity
of his hay. In big, clunky letters
on a four-by-eight sheet of plywood,
he's sprayed the words Absolutely No
Trespassing, Don't Ask. Although he's
my neighbor, seeing him clattering along
alone on his tractor, I doubt we'll ever
speak. I respect his loud silence and allow
him his right to ignore me. He may be
a good man. Who knows? There may be a story
behind the sign. The drunken hunter
who shot his heifer. The stranger with permission
who left the gate open. His favorite mare
found dead on the road. Who knows?
Maybe his good-life dream turned to dust
like overplowed land, and not knowing
who to blame, he blames us all in bitter orange.
Or the sign means nothing more than what it says.
The loud, ugly letters just the product
of an unpracticed hand. He used to bale
his hay but this year raked it into one

big mound to mold. Mold's a rightful owner.
So are the geese and whitetails that graze
behind the sign. This spring the whole field,
as if to signify essential beauty, lit up,
claimed by a pair of sandhill cranes.

Shooter's Poetics

I just shot an oyster.
    I glance at the shadow
        in the corner.

I feel no guilt
    whatsoever.
        Oysters

are a buck and a quarter
    a shot. One oyster
        in a shot glass

rather than a shell.
    A guy at the piano bar
        is singing Stevie Wonder,

"My Cherie Amour."
    He's white, trimmed goatee,
        a little gray

at the temples.
    Pretty good voice,
        but not Wonder's.

He plays the piano
    well. No one appears
        to be listening.

Piano bar singer
        has an odd job,
                works in a kind of solitude

amid crowds
        who know he's just
                background music.

Still,
        it's not a bad job.
                Jon Sandoval.

His name
        in pink chalk
                on the board behind him.

I'll clap
        at the end of the set.
                People at the bar

are clearing out.
        Must be the end
                of happy hour.

Jon Sandoval
        quits the piano.
                The waitress and I clap.

He punches a tape
     and Terence Trent D'Arby comes on,
          a better singer,

but it's not the same.
     After awhile
          a party of five comes in

and Jon comes back,
     picks up the guitar,
          settles himself on the stool,

and hits a chord.
     The shadow in the corner,
          who's been here all along,

says, "Country Road, James Taylor."
     Loud. And it's a shot,
          not a request.

Jon looks at the guy,
     "You must be
          a mind reader, man."

To a Woman on the Local News

Dressed in jailhouse orange,
you explained to the judge
you thought you were fleeing Satan's agents
in those flashing cars. You explained
how your boyfriend dumped you
and took up with a witch. You knew
he didn't know what he was doing,
but when you went over to straighten him out,
she put a curse on you, and they'd been
after you ever since. From Florence
to Lolo, you eluded them with hard driving.
You'd seen enough chase scenes
to know it could be done.
The sheriff cleared the way ahead
and laid a carpet of nails across
the road. Two tires blew, but you were scared
and kept that U-Haul floored
around the bends and down the straightaway
for Missoula. At the corner of Reserve
and Purgatory, you made a hard left
into the roadblock that slowed you down
enough for one of them to break out
your shotgun window before you slammed
a patrol car out of your way
and headed across town toward the Interstate.
I wonder if the judge believed
even part of your story? I wonder
if you realize now the man
who shot out your last two tires
and finally ran you off the road

was working for the other side?
On TV you fluffed your hair and asked,
"Am I gonna be on TV?"
Your mad eyes and girlish smile
hit me like a truck, and I fell for you,
though you looked like hell.
Where are you now? What happened
to your boyfriend and the witch?
We never got the whole story. It was never
clear where you were going. Are they
watching you in Warm Springs? Are you
closed in a cell replaying your wildest day
like a bad movie that keeps ending
with someone like you lying on a bed
of nails? Or are you out of jail,
looking now out of someone else's eyes?

Letter to Simmerman from Simmerman's Office

Jim, in this room without windows, it makes
perfect sense that you've covered these
institutional blue walls with every lively poster,
photo, and postcard you could find: Are You
a Punk? Is This What We Voted For? Dreamland
Candy Shop, and the smallest poster of all,
Poetry against the End of the World.
There's a struggle here to keep off the gloom,
to let some light in.

Lately I leave the door open, the door
where for some reason of your own,
you've hung the French flag. Maybe
you wanted to let those who enter here
know they are entering a foreign country.
Maybe you were thinking Bastille. Or maybe
you just wanted some color. Usually the talk
in the halls is in Spanish, ¡En español,
por favor, no inglés! That was one of the languages
in the air here before this building enclosed
the space. The Havasupai, Hopi, and Navajo
walk down the hall saying phrases nearly as old
as what the ravens say as they sit on the roof
of the gymnasium that overlooks the parking lot.
One day I understood a raven to say, "Walk in beauty,
friend." Another day it was, "Squawk, squawk."

Last week they painted the traditional greetings
from sixteen languages on the wall of the third-
floor hall. Now it's easier to tell one end
of this building from the other. If you come
from the north, turn left at Buon Giorno
and you'll be back in your office where little
has changed. Yá át ééh, the Navajo say.

Remember Arnette, the black janitor from Detroit?
He was so humble and well mannered some people
thought he was retarded. He and I were becoming
good friends, then a new janitor took his place.
Arnette's story, like much of what I read here,
is unclear, something about a fight with his wife
that led to a fight with his neighbor who shot
Arnette on the front lawn. No one knows where
he's gone. You ought to know that the new janitor,
who enters the office in the evening to pick up
the trash, doesn't knock.

There's Always Been a Place for Good Writing,
one of your posters declares. And next to that,
The Ink Spots in concert. On the wall above,
The Marines Are Looking for a Few Good Men,
and the good men and women of Guatemala march
in the streets above the words People and Students
Struggling for Freedom. I appreciate the logic
of the small world you've made of these walls.
I love the kind face of the Valedictorian Dog.

We stare at each other in dignified silence
in the late afternoons, along with the other dogs:
the mad one, the thumb sucker, the cowboy,
the big-nosed professor, the winking skull-face,
and the student dogs asleep on their books.

The Big One

The ex-all-pro tight end
is flying over my house again.

He's having such a good time
you'd think he'd died and gone to heaven,

doing stalls, dutch rolls, mini-astronauts
to feel the g force, something like

a diving catch on the one. The cows
as usual are puzzled, the horses

would applaud like regular fans
but they are overcome by shyness

and lack of hands. Then the wind comes up.
The same wind that pushed the glaciers

and would like to do it again, when the time
comes. So he has to set the plane

down on the field just right
and get back into the TV that used to be

his home, and fasten his seat belt
and sit there with all the others,

dream-circling that fogged-in terminal in another state
where the relatives wait.

Now it's just the wind and me warming up, stretching,
getting ready for the real, the true, the big one.

PART FIVE

Ruins

Dream **E**aters

The javelinas have come down the wash again
    from their hidden place
near Catclaw Mountain where the spring
    appears and disappears
and tinajas fill when it rains.
    Nearly blind,
working their snouts along the ground,
    bristling in their musk
with spines in their jowls, they pass the old stone walls
    of the ranch house,
the roof beams long ago carried off by scavengers,
    the windows broken
by boys throwing rocks or shooting
    at ghosts
adrift in the rooms, the pipes warped
    and slowly rusting,
the windmill fallen on the rocks, bones
    among the bones
of saguaro, the blades like a great parched sunflower
    facing the sun,
or the stars of the Big Dipper pouring dust,
    or the lowered, curious faces
of a band of small-eyed pigs known to certain children
    as dream eaters.

They have come to my window on the West
    that touches the desert floor
to eat the birdseed and potato skins. A boar,
    two sows, and four piglets

about the size of the Colorado river toads
    that sometimes come
in their venomous green skins to stare down
    their reflections
like rivals in the glass. But the piglets
    look harmless,
and I, childless, would like to pick one up
    and hold it
in my arms, sing maybe, or tell a story
    about a family and a ranch
and the ones that live in the mountains
    and eat whatever they find there.

New York, New York

The young bartender smiled and said hello when the four of us
   walked in to the Monte Vista Lounge. There was a Navajo
   couple at the bar leaning over their drinks, heads close together,
   talking quietly. A couple of students sat in a booth with books
   and notes spread out on the table before them. The rest of the
   place was empty. I stopped at the jukebox and played "New
   York, New York" for Bill, who was homesick, then I saw
   myself in the wall mirror at the far end of the lounge dancing
   up like a cheerful, slightly drunk friend.

   Judy and I were hungry, but the cook had closed up and gone
home, so we ordered another pitcher of beer and some pork
rinds. When the pitcher was empty, we strolled out into
downtown Flagstaff, which at nearly midnight on Wednesday
was all but deserted. The air was still. What streetlights there
were shone dimly at the corners, and we could see the handle of
the Big Dipper glittering above the dark shape of the Monte
Vista Hotel. We stopped for a red light at the corner, although
there were no cars coming.

   On the next block across the street, a tall, thin man came
running awkwardly out of the alley and down the sidewalk.
Someone on a bicycle turned the corner out of the alley and
rode in pursuit. I watched their black silhouettes against the
storefront glass as the bicycle pulled alongside the thin man and
the rider leapt, tackled the man around the shoulders like a
bulldogging cowboy, and wrestled him to the sidewalk. The
bicycle fell over the curb and slid into the street, wheels
spinning. For a moment, the two figures rolled as one on the
concrete. Then the shorter one pushed himself up and stood
over the thin man, kicking him as he writhed on the sidewalk.
Just as the thin man began to struggle to his feet, another man   71

ran up, kicked him once in the ribs, then grabbed his hair and began pounding his head on the concrete while the other man kicked at his hips and legs. I yelled something as loud and mean as I could and ran toward them, leaving my friends standing on the sidewalk. The two attackers ran off in separate directions.

The man lay sprawled on the sidewalk. When I bent over him, he flinched and his right hand went to his head as if to ward off more blows. It's alright, I said, they're gone. Are you okay? He looked stunned, as though his eyes wouldn't focus, but he wanted to get up. I helped him to his feet. He was unsteady and couldn't stand by himself. I led him to a corner between the door and display window of a shop. The masked face of a kachina figure stared out from the shop window, and behind it hung a Navajo rug with the intersecting lightning bolts of the storm pattern. The man was nearly a head taller than me, and when I looked into his face—a thin, sharp-boned Navajo face—I saw this wasn't the first time he'd suffered at the hand of another. He had a horizontal scar over his right cheekbone and another smaller scar on the bridge of his nose. His skin was weathered and stretched over the bones of his face, and his eyes were like two blackened dimes. His hair was thick and straight and raven black, and I guessed he was younger than the hard years that shone in his face. He stood still, dazed, and I brushed some dirt off his face and ran my hand lightly over his skull, which seemed unbroken. The only blood was a thin trickle from the hairline above his left temple. He smelled of stale beer and bar smoke. Are you okay? He shook his head and blinked his eyes. They rolled me, he said, and he took me by the arm and urged me to come with him into the alley. With one arm I helped support him, and together we staggered around the corner into the alley out of which, a few moments before, I had seen him run. I peered into the shadows for some movement or dark shape of a figure waiting in ambush.

He urged me again to go with him, and though he said nothing, I knew he was looking for something. I found a pair of dark glasses near an overturned garbage can, and a few steps farther by a Dumpster, I found a fifty-dollar bill lying on the gravel. Is this yours? He nodded as I handed it to him. We looked around some more but found nothing. He leaned back against a splintered phone pole and stared at the glasses and the fifty-dollar bill in his hands. We stood together in stillness in the dark for a moment. Stars shone above the alley and a train rumbled in the distance. Then we were fixed in a bright light, a light that is nearly always too late.

I walked out of the alley and across the street to where my friends were waiting. You'd have been murdered, Bill said, if you did that in New York.

After Anger Breaks up the Song

I walked for weeks in the cinder hills
along the basaltic bluffs
above the Río de Flag, up and down
the old paths between ruins
of pithouses, across the washes
and terraces where the ones the Hopi
call Hisatsinom, the ancient people,
tended their small plots of corn,
squash, and beans, where they walked
and sang the sun up and danced the rain
down from the mountains.
I dreamed their lives, those to whom
the land was sacred, to dream my own life
whole.

But to enter the dream, I had to walk
through a dying river, the water
polluted with heavy metals and human
waste. Someone put up signs with the word
Contaminated in red letters. But how
do we warn the robins that gather here
each fall by the hundreds to drink
on their way south, or the swallows
that nest in the bluffs and swoop
and glide fancy over the water
each twilight, or the elk that move
like ghosts through miles of cinder hills
to water here? Still the damaged waters

are not dead. Ask the robin that attacks
the red letters of the sign. After anger
breaks up the song, the thirst returns,
and the sun cracks jokes, and there's
laughter in the water loud as the heart's drum.

The Bluffs

There are two Navajo taboos concerning the coyote
    that stay in my mind. Don't bother a coyote
that takes the firstborn goat or lamb. It is his.
    It keeps order in the world. Don't cross the path
of a coyote. You will have bad luck. You will be in danger.

It was a hot, still day with a hard blue sky
    that didn't move at all. After watering the small
garden still in morning shadow, I worked upstairs
    at my desk, looking out the window, now and then,
at the cinder hills, Tufa, also known as O'Neil Crater,
    prominent among them, and the juniper- and piñon-
covered bluffs above the Río de Flag.

The dogs lay in the cool dirt under the porch
    waiting to hear the sound of my feet on the stairs,
waiting to go for their afternoon romp through the stream
    and over the bluffs into the cinder hills
to chase rabbits, squirrels, lizards, and whatever ghost
    scents lingered in the air.
This has been our ritual all year, these afternoon walks
    over the bluffs just east of Flagstaff
and north of old Route 66. Flagstaff Arizona, don't forget
    Winona. I sing sometimes, walking out of the house
made of cinder stones, built by Hopi masons, and later
    enlarged to house the road crew that paved the road.
It's the oldest house around, if you don't count the Sinagua
    ruins, the pithouses hidden all over the landscape
along the bluffs, on the ridges of the craters
    and under the lava flows.

There were people here long before 1066 when Sunset Crater
    was formed by the last eruption of this great
volcanic field, people who still spoke with the animals
    and knew how to grow corn, squash, and beans
in the rich ash. For hundreds of years they flourished,
    building larger and larger villages, great stone
houses, ceremonial kivas, and ball courts. Then they began
    to move or die of diseases or famine or war.
No one knows for sure. It's a mystery I walk in
    with the dogs in the afternoon, moving slowly among
the ruins, sitting down in the hollows where they worked,
    sang around fires, looked at the stars, and made love.
I know it was a hard life, but sometimes I feel the joy
    they must have felt walking these old paths
over the bluffs, sitting down to rest under a big juniper,
    listening to the commentary of jays or ravens,
or watching swallows or a big red-tailed hawk make visible
    the intricate currents of air. I've smelled the clay
and cedar scents on the breeze that comes up from the desert
    and haven't felt alone, or felt just alone enough.

In winter I've walked in the snow and lost my way
    for a time, then followed the tracks of animals
back down from the bluffs. I only needed to see the snow
    beneath my feet. Once snow was blowing down so hard
and fast it covered all the tracks. I stood still and listened
    until I felt in my bones the wind erasing, the snow
whiting me out, and I ran, scared foolish, but this time lucky.

In spring I found elk antlers and tracks coming from the stream
    and followed them until I saw three young bulls grazing,
then chasing each other in circles, bucking, fighting,
    kicking up their long legs, raising around them
a golden dust in morning light. They stopped, thrust
    their muzzles up, muscles in their big shoulders
flexing and quivering. They didn't run but moved off
    single file, gliding over the stream, up the rocky bluffs
without a sound, just a slight movement of morning light
    carried into the pines.

I saw that movement and that light again today, although
    it was late afternoon, and summer. Usually the animals
won't let you see them, but you can feel them watching
    or listening in the distance like eavesdropping gods.
Sometimes you can smell them, they're so close. But they keep
    out of sight. You have to be content to study their tracks,
like a hunter or a scholar, to poke a stick through their scat
    or droppings to see the bones, hair, and hard seeds.
You have to be content to finger the wisps of hair or fur
    stuck to branches or barbwire fences, to read the grass
and weeds along the paths, to squat down and sniff at the
    burrows
    and nests and hollows among the rocks, under trees,
to see who's been sleeping where. That's what the dogs and I
    were doing today when we saw the coyote drifting along
the rocks and under trees like a skinwalker, a Navajo witch.
    She stood up on her hind legs as though she meant
to address me in this act of imitation. The dogs put their ears
    and tails down and came bumping up against my legs.   **78**

I grabbed their collars and tried to calm them. I knelt down
    and held still, watching her. She turned around
in a full circle standing on her hind legs, an odd
    pirouette, a grim circus dog dancing, mocking
and being mocked, then dropped to the ground, sniffed the air,
    took two steps toward us, threw her head back, and howled.

The dogs answered her. I would have answered too, but I
    didn't have the voice for it, that voice I heard in my
bones. I remembered the second taboo and thought not
    of bad luck or danger but of respect for a space,
a privacy like a sister's. As we walked home down the bluffs,
    we could hear her voice changing through trees and rocks,
and it was as if the hills themselves were speaking.

For a year now, I've walked these bluffs. I've stooped among
    the ruins to look at shards of pottery, the old red
and black fired bowls and lips and handles of storage jars,
    and whiteware with black linear designs like Greek keys,
or figures of the maze that map the soul's journey, or single-
    line circles within circles, spirals of the infinite,
migration signs, the curved line of the snake, the parallel
    streaks of rain or shafts of sunlight breaking through
clouds, zigzags of lightning or thought, clear symbols of the
    elements that shaped their lives. I found arrow points,
manos and metates for grinding, tools for planting and hoeing,
    and once, a perfect stone axe.

I was bent down to look at the broken pieces of a bowl
    lying in the cleft of a rock. My hand was on its way

to a certain lip piece when I saw something, a curved shape
    I recognized, a stone phallus coming out of the earth
between rocks. I couldn't help myself, my hand reached for it
    and drew it out of its sheath of earth where it had
rested for thousands of years. I held it up, turned it
    in the light, an axehead, ground and shaped by hand,
smoothed out of hard stone, made to last. I could feel
    the hours, the days of work, the patience and care.
I could feel the smooth lines, the seriousness and the humor,
    the satisfaction and the weight, as I held it in my hand.
I could feel what he must have felt, the man who made it,
    part of him alive, still there in the stone,
and in the voice of the hills.

Blessing at the Citadel

By the time I had walked out of the canyon
toward the end of a day of deep quiet
and daydreams among lizards and wrens,
a day of clarity in the sun and puzzles
in the shadows where I found the petroglyph
of a running animal pecked into the rock
at the base of the canyon a thousand years ago,
the animal I thought at first was a horse,
but after looking awhile and thinking about it
realized was a mountain lion, I was ready
I thought for anything.

I was feeling strong, light, open.
I was ready to sing for a stranger,
or walk into the cinder hills with one
of the spirits of Lomaki, or put on a black
satin cape, step out of my dusty shoes,
croak, and flap off to ride thermals
with the ravens. I was that happy,
as if a new depth had entered my life.

When I came upon the tattooed family
posing for pictures among the walls and rubble
of Box Canyon Pueblo, and noticed
their station wagon with Indiana plates
and the trailer with the words Skin Tattoos
painted carefully in big black letters,
I considered asking the smiling father,
his tattooed belly bulging proudly beneath
his shirt, to make a portrait of the lion

on my chest. I was that happy.
But asked instead, How you doing?
Pretty good so far, he smiled.
And I went on walking across the road,
past a battered pickup, to Nalakihu
and the Citadel, home to the Hisatsinom,
ancestors of the Hopi, guardian spirits
of the land nicknamed America.

I suppose I should keep this to myself,
but there are things in a life that happen
only once and make us who we are,
like being born from one woman
or the first true kiss that makes
all the others possible. I suppose
I should hold my heart hostage
to a regular beat, and if it must go faster,
they say, it should do so gradually
so it isn't strained or damaged
so the whole system starts to break down
and the invisible bird that flies
back and forth between the extremities
bursts into a sudden scattering
of individual feathers.

But there they were, three of them,
standing at the top of the Citadel
in late afternoon light, silhouettes
among the rocks rising like gods
in human figures from the ancient walls.

I stood quietly on the trail below
until one of them came down to me
and put a hand on my shoulder, lowered
his head, opened my shirt, and spoke
in the old way directly to my heart.
Don't go any further heart, he said,
until you are blessed. He rubbed hooma
over my chest and touched my forehead
with the white dust of cornmeal on his fingers.
He poured hooma in my left hand
and placed a sprig of cedar in my right.
Go pray, he said. What for? I asked.
Pray for now, this place, all your relations.
Pray for the hostages.
Then he walked off down the trail
to join the others, not gods
but poor, living men from Moenkopi
here at the home of their ancestors
to pray for the world and bless a stranger.

The Iowa Poetry Prize Winners

1 9 8 7

Elton Glaser, *Tropical Depressions*
Michael Pettit, *Cardinal Points*

1 9 8 8

Mary Ruefle, *The Adamant*
Bill Knott, *Outremer*

1 9 8 9

Terese Svoboda, *Laughing Africa*
Conrad Hilberry, *Sorting the Smoke*

The Edwin Ford Piper Poetry Award Winners

1 9 9 0

Lynda Hull, *Star Ledger*
Philip Dacey, *Night Shift at the Crucifix Factory*

1 9 9 1

Walter Pavlich, *Running near the End of the World*
Greg Pape, *Sunflower Facing the Sun*